Ocean's Laughter

Ocean's Laughter

Poems by

Tricia Knoll

You are so smart!
and writ such great
people skills to keep
us on some sort
of path.

Tricia

Aldrich Press

Cover Art: Photography by Darrell Salk

ISBN 13: 978-0692541852

Kelsay Books
Aldrich Press
www.kelsaybooks.com

I thank many people for help with *Ocean's Laughter*. Kathleen Ryan and Mark Beach introduced me to Manzanita, Oregon and more. Gillian Galford Trevithick shared my joy in collecting pocket rocks and watching the play of dogs in surf. Darrell Salk walked many miles of shore with me.

I am grateful to scientists mentioned in the Notes. Poets at the Poetry Studio at the Attic Institute and Feral Cats workshop members (Shawn Aveningo, Cathy Cain, Carolyn Martin, and Pattie Palmer-Baker) helped with many poems.

Andrea Hollander taught me to tighten and assemble the poems into a sequence. A mentor.

Acknowledgements

Journals

About Place Journal, "Blessing the Fishing Fleet," "Ecologist on the Whale Watching Cliff"

Catch and Release — the Literary Blog of Columbia – A Journal of Literature and Art, "The Dead Warbler on My Welcome Mat"

Contemporary Haibun Online, "Wiping Up for Moving Out"

Dark Matter, "A Child's Sea Garden of Verbs"

New Verse News, "Prepared for the Big If," "The Loop at Nehalem Bay State Park," and "The Parts We Did Not See"

Orion Magazine's Tumbler website, "Apologies to the Former Owners of My Beach House" and "The Cottage Garden One Block Off the Beach"

Poplorish, "On the Cliff With Your Ashes"

Rain Magazine, "Pocket Rocks and Fondle Stones"

Spindrift Journal, "I Come Back Again and Again," "The Wreck of the Santo Christo de Bergos on Manzanita Beach, 1693," and "I Know Rain"

Stone Path Review, "Driftwood" and "On the Shore"

The Soundings Review, "Gravity Holds Me Hostage," and "September 12, 2001"

When Women Waken, "Tabloid Talk on the Hollywood Starlet"

Windfall – A Journal of Poetry of Place, "Manzanita Horses" and "Mid-Week Mid-Morning May"

Written River, "The Way The Wind Blows"

Anthology

Words Fly Away: Poetry for Fukushima, "Eye of the Tide" and "Tsunami Sea Glass"

The title, "Ocean's Laughter," is from Pablo Neruda's *Book of Questions,* Copper Canyon Press, translation by William O'Daly and is included as one line from Neruda's work in the poem "Mid-Week Mid-Morning May." Both used with permission of Copper Canyon Press. The map in "Mise en Scène — Manzanita, Oregon" is provided courtesy of Elk Ridge Publishing Company, Manzanita, Oregon.

Do you not also sense danger at the sea's laughter?

—Pablo Neruda, *The Book of Questions*

Contents

I Came Back Again and Again

to read *Crime and Punishment*
escape the lock-up ward
run full out on canted sand
hold a hand, fold a leash
laugh at knock-knock jokes
play Scrabble
make love on a rock-hard bed
hear my sump pump chuff
solve who-dun-its – which tenant broke three wineglasses
fly a white shark kite
study tide tables to sneak around Hug Point
hunt for green in sunsets
sniff limes
rummage for wineglasses at the recycle center
witness the bravado of wind kiters and surfers
ask what the ocean does with a dropped cell phone
listen to my mother's stories about my father
drink my first martini
replace rickety windows and a leaky roof
build a garden sunroom
bet on when stuck-up clouds blow off Neahkahnie
read the cinquains of Adelaide Crapsey
wish I could read what dogs find in gull prints
write haiku and letters to City Council
hunt for the perfect sand dollar
tickle sea anemones to squirt at me
bike the bay spit trail when scotch broom blooms
trudge in sand to the jetty to eat deli sandwiches on hot lava rocks
decipher sand scribbles of who loves whom before the tide shifts
feel wind in my hair

always wind in my hair

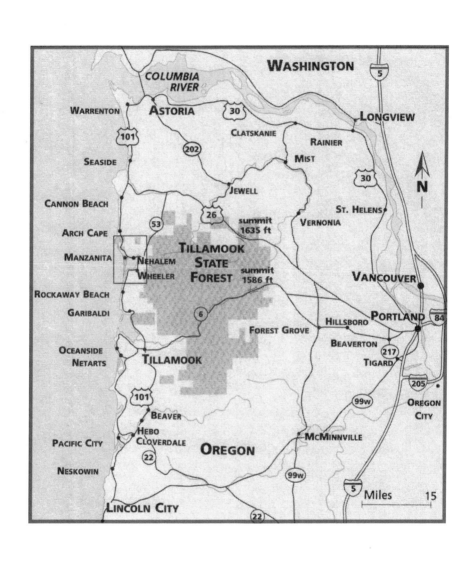

Mise en Scène – Manzanita, Oregon

Manzanita, Oregon is halfway between the North Pole and the equator, an emerald of temperate rain-forest on the Pacific Coast ring of fire. Tillamook County is home to Laurel Mountain – one of the rainiest places in Oregon. Life here breathes rain – 75 to 90 inches a year.

About 650 people live in Manzanita. Some homeowners rent to tourists or use their houses as second homes. The resident population consists of artists, merchants, people who work from home, and lots of retirees. Elections squeak in blue.

The town sits between two state parks. At the north end of Manzanita is Oswald West State Park. Governor West ensured that all Oregon beaches are public. This park boasts the highest coastal landmass between San Francisco and Canada, Neahkahnie Mountain (elevation 1,680 feet). The name may be a Tillamook tribal word for "where diety turned to stone." On a clear day, from Neahkahnie it's possible to see 28 miles to Cape Lookout, sometimes 65 miles to Nestucca and far into the ocean.

Seven miles south at the other end of the beach is Nehalem Bay State Park — 900 acres of dunes, grass, shore pines, and salal. Elk have chased boys on bikes on trails during rutting season. Eagles stand silhouette on driftwood. The Park rents spaces for bike and tent campers and RV's, and offers yurts. The 100-mile-long Nehalem River enters the Pacific from the bay behind the park. Fishermen chase runs of chinook and coho salmon.

People come to comb the beach – and may find flotsam from the Fukushima tsunami following the 2011 Tohoku earthquake. Or for clamming. Crabbing. Wave watching. Leaving behind other places.

Travel to Manzanita by car or bike, depending on whether Douglas firs, rocks or mud have slid onto Highway 101. This two-lane highway snakes around Neahkahnie mid-way up a cliff, past whale watching signs. By plane – there's a landing strip with a windsock at elevation 30 feet in the bay park. No control tower, fuel refill station or landing fee. A dock nestles inside Nehalem Bay.

In January 1700, an earthquake of at least a magnitude 9 ruptured the Cascadia subduction zone along 1,000 miles of coast from Northern California to Vancouver Island. The resulting tsunami struck Japan and swept over Manzanita. This fault lets go approximately every 350 years. It does not generate swarms of level 3 and 4 quakes over many years. Seismologists warn the fault is locked and loaded.

Longer ago than that, the Nehalem Tillamook people and some of the Clatsop tribe lived on this shoreline. They burned selected slopes to encourage browse for deer and elk and canoed north to the Columbia River before Europeans "discovered" it. Creatures (two-headed snake, horned rabbit, husbands wished from stars), potlatch, shipwrecks, fur trade, Spanish treasure, and an epidemic populate their stories.

Off Oregon's shores, including Manzanita, oxygen-low hypoxic waters have formed dead zones. Scientists study shifts in historic water temperatures, wind patterns and ocean currents due to climate change as well as acidification from increasing carbon dioxide levels. Part of the ocean depths are dying.

Ninety years ago Kahlil Gibran, the Lebanese-American poet, wrote of a different shore:

> *I am forever walking upon these shores,*
> *Betwixt the sand and the foam.*
> *The high tide will erase my foot-prints,*
> *And the wind will blow away the foam.*
> *But the sea and shore will remain*
> *Forever*

May it be so. More than twenty-five years ago, I bought a house on Beeswax Lane, one block south of Treasure Cove, and four blocks from where deer sometimes meander Manzanita's main street. My "Ocean Pines" paid its way with an ocean view and vacation rentals. Much comes and goes here.

The Way the Wind Blows

*The keeper of the Tillamook Rock lighthouse, on the coast of Oregon,
reports that in the winter of 1902 the water of the waves was thrown more
than 200 feet above the level of the sea, descending upon the roof of his
house in apparently solid masses.*
— D. W. Johnson from *Shore Processes and Shoreline Development*

We name flavors of rain —
haze, sleet, shower, sprinkle,
drizzle and deluge.

In winter winds,
umbrellas are useless.
Bring a hat in all seasons,
pull it down tight.

Some January waves slide perpendicular
to the shore. Sand scours eyeballs.
Less than ninety-hour-per-mile winds
— merely a good winter blow.

We measure weather
by how sand blows.
Summer sifts. Winter drifts.
High winds in the afternoon,
still at dawn or sunset.

Weigh cloud heft as mist,
fog or rain on Neahkahnie.

If the sun sets into licks of waves
rather than blanking out in cloud buffers,
it means a good night. Praise visible stars
and moon, night graces on a wave length.

The world could blow away,
drain away, or melt
at the whim of an angry sea.

I Know Rain

soft dimples in the gutter

sideways blows
that stoop the ocean pines

a wash-away of my sweat
when I run in a squall

to the overhang
outside the pizza place

you kissed me under an umbrella
cold water dripped

down the nape of my neck

Klaska – The Lost Clatsop Word for *They*

Tribes of Clatsop and Nehalem first people told each other stories during winter darks. Tales of Moon's two wives, escapades of Ice, Wild Woman's couplings, celebrations of roasted whales, the love dance of crow and seal, and South Wind slamming through winter, uprooting trees.

One winter South Wind met Ocean's daughter, fell for her, and offered to take his rampage-gifts to her father. She missed her soft ocean bed and went with him. He met Ocean's pets – whales and seals. He presented his rootwad cedars.

Much later, the people stood on sinking sand and stared toward the horizon – beyond the familiars of cloud, wave, rain, sun-glint, and mist. They saw a floating forest coming at them, a canoe with wings, a sea monster rising up from Ocean's realm, carried on the urging betrayal of South Wind.

*

A hundred years later a missionary wrote down these people's stories. Skimming in on the tide, the fair-skin sailors seemed to be cannibals, they told him, blood drained out. He wrote that the people might have squatted like frogs, *oh-ing* round vowels of frog people. He recorded how a young Nehalem woman saved a red-haired man from a shipwreck near Nehalem Spit. They begot red-haired, blue-eyed children. These stories he believed.

The tale he dismissed — *labored to reason them out of their folly*, he said — told of the anger that Captain Domanis, a trader, visited on the people decades later. Captain D received only small skins from them; their plusher pelts went to the Hudson Bay Company. So the captain nailed a rotten sail to a tree, uncorked a vial, doused the cloth with a liquid that unleashed an epidemic of ague on the land. Many, many people died.

Klaska, the lost Clatsop word for blame.

The Wreck of the Santo Cristo De Burgos on Manzanita Beach, 1693

The first people told of a Spanish ship
as they offered fur traders
chunks of beeswax, wax ballast
from Filipino bees, hauled for candles
for missions down south. A winter storm
blew the galleon north, evidenced in cobblestones,
Chinese porcelain shards,
and teak timbers scattered on the spit.

I live on Beeswax Lane. I've told children
how the wax floated to where the river
beckons salmon home, about those bits of a wreck
that carried Mexican silver to Manila,
how a tsunami took away the rest.

My sea-blood loves shifts in rippled sand,
watery glimpses of wave-wracked past.
Hunters of that lost ship and its legend of buried treasure
raise money to haul sonar, to tow detecting rigs,
to interpret arrows carved on stone. Their work
faces Neahkahnie's rock wall and unforgiving tides.
I hope they find the Santo Cristo.

Sorting and sifting,
the ocean wins.

All Loss Turns

on unpredictable clocks.

My doll's missing head.

A jade ring flung off with a garden glove.

A friend slept in her attic
the one night a cereus
bloomed in her solarium.

That boy missing for twenty-one years,
whose body surfaced in a shallow grave.

Fukishima timbers in the currents
swiping the shore.

September 12, 2001

This coast, far west and away,
a windless shroud of fog bellies down,
smothers dune grass and pulls up chill
the morning after.

Mist walkers, hazy down the beach,
torsos in motion, settle footprints against
outgoing tide. Seen through the lens of faraway,
they disappear into the wet, sun-bleared golden lost.
Joggers and dogs stay home.
There is television.

Squinting through my misted glasses,
sand cities appear, one after another,
rounded humps and lumps of medieval fortresses,
the most sand towers ever
on this beach where ambitious tides
sluice away moats in the first wash.

Small hands sculpt grainy turrets and bucket buildings
with black water-smooth stone windows.
Mothers and fathers, shovels in hand,
pat foundations. Families together
as the tide retreats
in fog's privacy.

A white clam-shell fence circles
a sand-dripped goddess sanctuary
paved with unbroken sand dollars.
Gull feather flags lean.

Be Brave. Big Wave.

We said these words
to the wide-open low tide
under May's yellow sun.

Your father held your left hand.
I had your right. Three of us wading
with cold toes.

The curve of the wave
ached to arch
into that second of time,
one beat of a baby's eyelash.

You winked your blue eyes
above the white of a milk-tooth smile.

At the turning reach of a minus tide,
scalloped cross hatches
thinned and thrived
to sink in sand.
So simple
it seemed

that spring day
we three held hands
and went to sea
with our lives.

On the Shore

I follow a young mother in jeans
who runs to keep up.
Her toddling son lurches
across rippled sand.

Look, she says, *Patterns!*
The child jogs, mooshing
wave-lapped ridges beneath sneakers
flashing blue lights.

Stacked clouds —
a god to the east,
fish-scales to the west,
and mist draping the mountain.

Wave battalions advance.
We flee an assertive one.
Brown pelicans skim the trough
in a line.

Repetition
in clam dimples,
footprints of gulls.

What does the boy understand?

We breathe the same mist,
walk the vast splattered sand,
measure the tide's retreat
in abandoned snakes of sea foam.

His feet trudge
one after another,
head tucked low

over skeleton-studded sand.

Pocket Rocks and Fondle Stones

For GGT, geologist.

Her toddler's hand plucked up
the first fondle stones
as sparkles in salt water,
green or black basalt pennies.
We squirreled them in pockets
gritty with sand, pinched
them in place to pave
our garden's path with rock money.

Hand warmers, flatnesses
and worry stones for a thumb's ease.

She understands each,
veined or water tumbled,
like nothing else on earth, singularities,
jewels juxtaposed with scents
of barnacles, brine, kelp, sand, and sea.

Those pocket rocks grew
to bowlfuls; a cracked yellow
cookie mixing bowl, last of a graduated set,
stainless steel pressure cooker from Goodwill,
white enamel stewing pot.

I house old bowls
of bold stones. Mother keeper
of the rocks.
A hand need never be empty or alone.

Manzanita Horses

The tourists unload vans. Haltered stall creatures
sniff the salt and stamp their hooves,
wind flaring their manes, nostrils
tickled at kelpy scents of ancient and clean.

Families ride from the jetty at Nehalem Bay
to the foot of Neahkahnie Mountain, six miles
past homes of Nike millionaires and drafty cottages
handed down from one generation to the next,

the horses with names like Whirlwind and Whisk,
appaloosas, quarter-horse crosses,
mixes of Tennessee walkers
and saddle-breds, leaving

half-moon footprints and green scum
in the swash. A dalmation barks.
An unleashed pug harasses the prancers
who test salt water on winter-furred legs.

Manzanita horses were the passwords we held
secret, my daughter and me.
Words for safety.

Driftwood

A June storm wet the driftwood last night
presenting sanded trees as silvered salt relics.
They rolled in the tide.
Slain dragons and griffons.

Today the beach is a gallery
of fir leg bones and cow skulls,
arks of barnacles and shipworms.

I am small, foot-bound
where surf flings forward
this feeble fence on a slumming dune.

Root wad fingers spike up.
One skeleton clutches
a boulder in its roots
for the last touchdown.

Wind carves. Sand blasts.
Waves rearrange. The ocean knows
its delivery rules.

What is big
will be small or gone,
char in bonfires.

Pacific Night Work

We settled with the sun into bed last night,
after walking sand into darkness, thinking
we heard Japanese temple bells, feeling
crumbled styrofoam under our bare feet,
tsunami debris from sea-swept homes.

A child's shovel is not safe
stuck in sand overnight. Mornings
light up a new beach, handiwork
of the cleaner, scrubber, rearranger
of rootwad benches.

Tucking back from the rising wind,
at dawn it seems a giant vacuum sucked out
the footprints left between sand castle
and swash line, wringing
feather flags from shifting
sandy battlements.

It is true. Tides' scrubbed-sand carpets
arrange up ripples, swirls,
air bubbles of clams. Moon-drenched
waves sprinkled the tidepools with food,
like night custodians who tend saltwater
tanks in the offices of oncologists.

O Pacific, you left gifts, tips
of crab legs while we napped
under the rinsing moon
rocked in rumbles
of your cleaning cart's wheels
spinning on wavering tracks.

As For Shopping

There's no hurry, for there's nowhere to go and nothing to buy.
—Harper Lee, *To Killing a Mockingbird*

Slow we go, but in Manzanita you can buy

bestsellers — mysteries, thrillers, Billy Collins and Neruda
chapstick, cheddar cheese, chanterelles, and crystal unicorns
duplicate keys, Dungeness crab, doorknobs, and dangle earrings
exit signs and enchiladas
frozen peas, fair trade chocolate, fudge
halibut, Haitian metal work, clothing made of hemp
Israeli clogs
knitting needles and kites
local produce and local brews, lifejackets made for dogs
massages, morels, marshmallows, and miniature lighthouses
nouveau, vegan, and organic cuisine
Parcheesi, pecorino romano, paper kites, postcards, and pinot noir
raspberry-glitter nail polish, razor clams, and roofing nails
sunscreen, spring chinook, Stumptown espresso, salt water taffy
Tillamook Mudslide ice cream
Yaquina bay oysters, yarn of silk
whole-grain bread and wind socks

You cannot buy

beeswax, bail bonds, barbecues, brand new beds or bonsai trees
cars, Chinese takeout or cell phones
diamond rings, DNA tests, dentures
gasoline, gin, or gluten-free matzo
haircuts, hearing aids
Indian fry bread
labradoodles
parakeets

34

scotch, sloe gin or succotash
tranquilizers, televisions, tuxedos, tattoos or timeshares
U of O sweatshirts
vodka

Tide tables are free. Newspapers sell out early.

The Refindery

The Unicorn, speaking of children, says to the King's
Messenger, *I always thought they were fabulous monsters!*
and asks about Alice, *Is it alive?*
 —Lewis Carroll, *Through the Looking Glass*

In the middle of the dunes and Scotch broom, close enough to hear the surf tumble but buffered from winter winds, is the waste transfer station known as CartM – dumpsters, recycle bins, and the Refindery, a store selling cast-offs. A witch soddered from gutter runs, rebar, and bottle stoppers, sports breasts of rusted funnels. Her toothless rake points to the parking lot. A broomstick-boned scarecrow in cement-filled, flat-tire shoes waves a ratty Stetson hat.

Cabin fever brings me out to eavesdrop. On chitchat, lifeblood about who showed up for ribs at the Sand Dune, the Spanish teacher who drank too much and whose car knocked over the fire hydrant near the pizza parlor. A dump for hot tips, settling scores, loose-lip news.

For four bucks, I buy two taupe candles with black wick tips, a half package of gold tissue paper, two monarch butterfly cards, one yellow pillowcase, three matching pinot glasses, and a blue mason jar. I try out the stiff stationary bike whose odometer reads several thousand miles. I do not buy the red-and-black enameled tin box – its gold label from a pet crematorium pays respects to Princess.

The floor-to-ceiling cardboard box smasher revs up. Two black labs by the roll-away door growl. The man running the compactor yanks off his ear protectors, scolds. The dogs slink off to gray blankets beyond a sagging pink-and-green floral couch.

Turning, I see the unicorn. White with a gold horn. A frayed pink metallic ribbon collar. Wedged into the side of a handmade case of musty books, it's a plush book-end, smudgy, one rear leg loose. Her hoofs and alicorn are plastic. When I pick it up, the dogs' tails brush dust. Throw and fetch, retriever dreams.

A rabbinical story tells how Noah had no more room when a unicorn approached the ark. He tied a rope around its neck and towed it in his wake. In time, it drifted.

This unicorn, smaller than a wastebasket, once loved-alive, arrived here for a second chance. I push the unicorn deeper into the shelf to keep it warm and dry behind a fence of a Nehalem tribal history text, a tattered dictionary of rhyme, and seven volumes of Proust.

City of Manzanita Lost & Found – Winter 2014

one hooded pink rain jacket, size small
a fluorescent-yellow broken umbrella
two sweatshirts (one U of O, one OSU — extra larges)
lime green flip-flops
three rings (ruby, gold band, and child-sized mood ring)
ten sets of household keys
one Prius key ring
one Kindle
a corkscrew
a surf rod and reel
two unmatched earrings
one pair of cat-eye sunglasses
four smartphones

Mid-Week Mid-Morning May

Weary-making winter winds have died.
The sidewalks start to unroll summer.
Two young men in overalls paint the trim
white on the salt-weathered cedar-sided
yoga - massage studio. The fair trade shop
flies its earth flag, three stars-and-stripes
hang limp at the post office, grocery store
and community center. Sales of winter
snuggle-clothes festoon the sidewalks,
hangered kites that sway like old women's skirts.
May ratchets up the rumble of RVs
crossing to Nehalem Bay dunes.

For the first time since October, the newspapers sell out.
There's only day-old doughnuts in the grocery store.
This morning's silver mist tempts
me to trust the glitz of sunlight's promise
that life gets better, sweeter.

SOLVE volunteers have swept the beach
of tsunami styrofoam and ruined shoes,
bits of blue fishing-boat rope,
the cigarette butts. Sleepy pillow clouds
hold out on the mountain for afternoon wind.
A bossy raven yanks out the purplish liver
of a gut-open gull. Ten crows hover.
Gulls eat anything. Others eat dead gulls.

The surf shop discounts wet suits (mostly smalls),
sail kites and marshmallow shooters (30 minis
in a reload). The peacekeeper model costs

three times more than the camouflage, shoots
a sure thirty feet in dune grass war games.

I buy Neruda's *Questions*
at Cloud and Leaf. *Do you not also sense
danger in the sea's laughter?*

Blessing the Fleet

Garibaldi, Oregon

You might have noticed
many things that May morning.
Light rain. Kids fumbling,
grumbling over life jackets,
the captain's dirty Pirates' cap,
how he watches the widow's walk
down the pier, hesitating to step up
on his deck, lilacs on her arms.

How we shift our bright baskets, making room
for orange azaleas, purple rhododendrons,
store-bought red carnations,
pink camellias, daffodils and dogwoods.

This may not have been the best day,
        showers buckling down,
but it is the way we remember
        waves criss-crossing Tillamook Bay.
Churning smell of diesel. Seagulls squawking.

Outside the harbor buoys, the captain slows
the motors inside the bar to open ocean.
Our small village drops branches overboard
one bud at a time to an overcast sea,
to bless this season's fleet
and the fishing.

        Names are read
        to honor the dead fishermen
        lost at sea.

A baby squalls. The captain tracks
where currents seize blossom
floats and crab pot buoys.

The widow's lilacs linger, drift.
She whispers one dear name
leaning out to fathoms, conjuring him
in gray-blue shadow spray,
churning purple blooms in her wake
of yesterday's retreating sea.
        So the names are said.

The Dog Store on the Main Drag

I guessed it would never succeed.
High-end real estate less than a block
from the beach. I was wrong.

People bring dogs that chase waves, shake,
slobber, dig quarries, and harass shorebirds.
Voilà – Manzanita's pet emporium, more dog than cat.

The shopkeepers do not stock the kibble my dog eats.
I don't need porcelain bowls stamped with green bones,
orange flotation jackets, red sweaters,
or rhinestoned cloaks with snaps for pups and poodles.

One October a homemade pumpkin biscuit
shaped like a fire hydrant.
That treat was a storm surge of affection for my dog
who listened when I demanded she not chew
a stranded dead seal. Another time homeopathic
anxiety drops, expensive, that did not stop her panting
in the car. My rescue bitch thinks
motors mean Animal Control
coming to sweep her up, carry her away.

Last night's storm blew a new dune
onto the wheelchair ramp
to the beach. We're headed out of town.
The surf is higher than I've seen in years.
I ask the dog to settle in the back seat.
She smears worry slobber across her window.

Lights go off in the dog store
hunkered in the upshore fist
of the next tsunami's waves.
Sweep up. Carry away.

Undertows of Spirit

One Bible church, one Veteran's cemetery,
a small town parade on the Fourth,
midwives at birthings,
the shamans of raucous gulls.

The dead wash in — seals, jellyfish, gulls,
pelicans, cormorants, sanderlings and stilts.

The dead float away.
Beware of wind. It lifts sifted cremains.
Bits of bone ride the tide
beside the driftwood.

This church of infinite outlooks,
sand, finite old-growth, tidepools,
prayer flags on the mountain top,
rock cairns and bonfire rituals

is open day and night
washed in sea salt.

Sand Script

I walk to the beach over tar-patch
on sun-bleached asphalt, its squiggles,
winter's telltales of heaved up,
and ice-coated dune grass pencils,
scribbles of cold sleet,

a tale of long-time licks,
waves' tongue stories in the neap tide

    cloud visions
    thorn tangles
    quartz-striped rocks
    seagrass snarls
    and rust.

This mist mess
scrawls scant passwords,
mirages in sand,

    time4us
    2longgone
    dontleaveme
    befairorbeware

unlocking what pushed me
out into beach combing.

A leaping gull, wind-steady,
holds a place. Caesura.
Threat clouds out west.

That April Day

You were silent, deep in your head, music making.
Our walk in mist, patches of blue over silver-gray
wet sand. Sun shafts set spotlights where the dunes shifted.
Your chin nodded to your new melody.

Your gloved hands twitched with chords.
The dead horse floated, legs up, bloat of barrel body.
Stiff legs from tapered stifle to the hoofs.
A black horse bobbing in sea foam.
Your black baby-grand piano upside down.

There are signs all over this beach. *Dangerous undertow.*
Sneaker waves. Beware rolling logs. Arrows to high ground.
We've seen pulled-unders, helicopter life-flights
for people washed out, coast guard lights at night.

The mother's shrill yell as a toddler tests chill water.
Stories of run-a-grounds. The Peter Iredale,
a four-master keeled up north in 1906, rib cage of rust.
Bad fogs. Bitter-cold squalls. Winter winds so stiff

we can't stand straight, and you're sand-blind.
I knew all this, even in April. What I didn't know
was how little you would care about that dead horse
on its back with ebony piano legs.

It might have been a beauty.

Blown Free in Warm August Wind When It Came to Naming Seashore Creatures

Sand dollars,
sea urchins,
sea stars,
razor clams,
by-the-wind-sailors,
the jellies of moons,
the lens of the lion's mane.

Dogwinkle shells
with horny operculums.

And crabs
in the eelgrass
from Dungeness.

Vellella vellella

These jellyfish, called by-the-wind sailors, float
raucous swells, a genetic tilt that sail them one way,
either west or east
spinning in storm swirls,
until stranded in the swash line
of March, to die on a beach.

Royal purple-blue, sun bleaches them
transparent like doused messages that lose
ink and urgency, the thinnest paper
of flat left or right slant sails, slow-erasing hints

    of waywardness
    go-where-the-wind pleases
    free sail.

Predetermined in birthright
of a diagonal sail,
eating what hovers below,
floating with your kind,
beaching in your time.
There are worse ways to live.

The Child's Sea Garden of Verbs

Children slosh in red plastic boots.
They pry, splash, dance back from rising waves,
and line their pockets with sticks and shells, things that smell.

Parents and grandparents tiptoe through a tidepool glossary to
conjure in marine garden, repeating names like spells.
Verb gifts of watch for sneaker waves and mind where you step.

a·nem·o·ne –   *Yawns open as a bloom on high tide to sip surf,*
uh-nem-uh-nee   *curls up at low tide. Remember where Nemo*
                  lives? Poke and squirt.

bar·na·cle –   *Touch the crust. I love you like a barnacle*
bar-nuh-kel   *loves the rocks, whales and sea-bound ships.*

bull kelp   *A jump rope! That bulb floats like a bathtub*
bull kelp   *toy. People used to collect it for food and*
                  fertilizer. Now we let it grow — a forest where
                  creatures hide. See the bugs?

                  Smell it? You'll know this as Oregon coast for
                  the rest of your life.

                  Whip the driftwood, not your brother.

lim·pet –   *Does it look like a tiny hat? Or something*
limpit   *else? Let it stick to your fingernail!*

mus·sel –   *Their shells make good shovels and sand castle*
muss-el   *windows and doors — you can eat the insides.*
                  (If you want to.) No pressure.

sea lettuce –   *Sniff the slime? You're right — rocks with*
see!-let-us!   *green hair. Some people eat this too!*

This, the language lab for sea hands.

Sea Stars

Five-finger lessons
how slow a starfish moves,
purple, red and orange ornaments
in rock-black crevices
mimicking night and the human hand.

From San Diego to Vancouver,
sea stars are dying.
Star wasting disease, the waste of stars.

The moral of that fable of a woman dancing?
She tosses one beached starfish back into the churn,
making a difference one at a time.

What ends a wish upon a fallen star
when there are no more?
One at a time.

The Gray Whale

See the rolling backs,
migrations passing these rock cliffs

that centuries asserted into the sea
beside certainties that gray whales

lift up their babies,
play by our boats,

migrate north and south, rise
for air, dive

for food,
survive the hunt,

and swallow sea-gut tortures
of hoses, baggies, balloons,

duct tape and rubber gloves.

Tabloid Spotlight on the Hollywood Starlet

As if sadness is a heroine, as if sadness
requires polaroid sunglasses to cool down
all-white glare, as if sadness demands
a shopping opportunity on Robertson Boulevard,

the headline says she was caught candid
on the boutique street, shopping bag dangling.
Without her newborn, her legs, lifted in heels, line up
to stretch her thighs to thin, tan advantage.

Blonde hair feathered like a sleek Sussex hen,
head bowed, her eyes hidden in wrap-arounds
are maybe blue, brown, possibly red. Her agent outed
her baby's wailing, her post-partum sadness,

a lonely fight to keep herself upright, walking.
The caption says her next role is a mermaid,
daylighted under water, shimmering, a breathing
tube, treading water in flukes of green scales,

trying to save the baby of a gray whale
tangled in tossed-off fish net, ribboned in kelp.

The Big If on Nehalem Bay Spit

Twenty years ago a snowy plover explored
the bay spit to find a nesting place. A June day
when one palm-size trilling wader
poked for shore flies, scooted
on stick-black legs on the scruff
of a minus tide.

Perhaps I didn't notice.

Were nester-plovers to show up now,
State rules say
        NO horseback riding, kite flying, dogs,
        bicycles, sand sails, beach volleyball,
        kites above the tide line.

Back-up plans
include placing poisoned eggs to kill
crows and ravens that gobble
plover eggs. Rope out birders.

One commissioner complains
of limiting family fun.
Another fears phone calls.

The betting at the bar
is the plover will be a no-show.

High Wind Power Outage

Strap on head lamps
like miners scuffling

on carpets of coal. Enter each room
to a flickerless switch,

mere habit of walking,
mere notions of sight

where I left clogs, notebooks,
my mother's necklace of garnet beads

in disarray, fallen to the dog's blanket.
A cell link

to the electric company hotline
that doesn't know the cause,

the location of the blowdown,
when it will end, how cold it will get,

who suffers the most,
what will be lost.

For security reasons
the girl-computer names only

numbers in our address,
not our street, nor our stress

where we walk shiftless
through our hallway tunnel to bed,

your hand pulling mine.

After The Storm That Took the Power Out

Logs dangle on rock levee lips near the river's mouth,
pick-up sticks big as freight cars, silver-medaled
in barnacles. Forest to river to sea to beach.

Men with pick-up trucks and chainsaws
slice up driftwood, firewood
for when power lines fall next time.

Tree debris is my zoo – a giraffe neck,
winsome grasshopper, hook-billed hawk,
the dragon with branching wings
and barbed tail.

I shoot pictures
of the slaying of the wyvern.

Letter to the Governor of Oregon

Please jumpstart an Oregon State Parks' study about cars cruising on Oregon's beaches.

Current Park policies prohibit cars and trucks during nesting seasons. Frequently during "open beach," people with chainsaws cut up driftwood for firewood, many without permits. This is illegal in Oregon — but unenforced because of limited patrol staffing. Tourists twirl sand wheelies.

A State Park's official confided to me that he thinks driving on the beach is a hangover from decades when mail was delivered in wagons down stretches of coast. When no one thought we could reduce shorebird numbers. Beaches are not soft-sand highways.

Wild spaces glimpsed through a windshield are not the same as smelling, seeing, feeling them. Allow beach access for people with mobility disabilities and for emergency responders.

Let's talk. Let's walk. Not joyride.

Letter #32 to the Manzanita City Council about Bonfires on the Beach

The City's recent water bill asked for input to Council on local issues. Here I am. Begging again for driftwood awareness.

High tides deliver these wave-tumbled sculptures to our beach. Today I saw a rampant locust, a boa with a rat in its belly.

Some say bonfires hold together gatherings to drink beer and roast marshmallows and hot dogs. I see isolated blazes trailing smoke for nameless tiny "tribes" up and down open beach. Tribes that want nothing to do with each other. There's evidence of an inverse relationship: the bigger the fire, the younger the fire starters.

We do not treat mountain wilds this way – is there anywhere more inhospitable to human trail-making than Oregon's beaches?

Each summer morning. Black scabs. Crust on sour char. Like smoking a Tiparillo at the tomb of the unknown soldier and stubbing it in a drinking fountain.

Others say beach fires are both mythic rite and right. A throwback to Vulcan who discovered a fisherman's fire on a beach, tucked it in a clamshell, and claimed flame as his own. Northwest first people lit flares on Cascade Head to call salmon to spawn in the Salmon River. Tribes here called driftwood Ocean's gift. South Wind's too. Rain seldom falls a second season on washed-up silver bristles or homeless rootwads. We burn them.

Find my permit application and check to hold a public event:

The Ocheaehoh Cheso (Tillamook for Come Ashore)

Sunday, July 5 at noon

A tai-chi-on-the-beach celebration,
 a community wave-in to invite timber
out of the tidal rocking chair. Come witness
for the final resting place of wood.

Enjoy Tillamook Fireside S'Mores ice cream and
huckleberries. Fly gray whale and starfish kites.

Join me. I'll be at the Treasure Cove access ramp, waving my arms.

This Space

Six miles of crossed wood bedded in sand,
sea-graced logs, a climbing gym
rolled over, up and over, over again.

Hunker here out of sandblow.
Tell your story about first love.
Your chair back is a tree trunk,
a windbreak west of the dune grass.

Cozy onto a double-wide
wood couch for coupled napping.
Soothe the contours of your spines
on voyager logs.

Rest your prayers on stout pews.
Touch the reliquary of bones,
rainforest silvered in salt.
Look west

from these landmarks
to the ceasefire belt
between deep breath
and spent trees surfing.

The Parts We Did Not See

What did we not see when
he bought a simple rope
    at the hardware store in Wheeler,
    testing hemp for stretch, for breaking point

when he showed it to his neighbor
    bragging about what a good rope
    it would be for all kinds of purposes
    at a fair price

or when he took it home and wound it
    around his brass bedpost, then around the newel
    on his stairway and pulled back
    as if water skiing on gray carpet

and when he scolded the dog for chewing
    the end of it before he wrapped the stub
    in duct tape?

Then when he climbed the stairs
    to the dusty attic and shook his head
    at the wicker bird cage
    and the brown cardboard suitcase his mother used
    for thirty years, filled with yellowed linens,
    her will, and smudged birth certificates
    of siblings he outlived

when he pulled out that three-legged maple stool
    his sister had used for milking
    or said she used for milking

and he looped the noose
    bragging to the dog
    that he could hang him too

if the mutt didn't stop nipping heels
and ripping the screen door

and how was it that volunteer firefighters
arrived seconds before he kicked out
that stool?

Tsunami Sea Glass

Saki glass whirls
of sea-glass green
marked Japan
and timbered posts
connect-the-dots.

Bath slosh rim to rim
high there, low here
back to us.

Yellow foam
of construction debris
sticks on my shoes.
Radioactive?

Flayed wallets yawn.

Juice bottles and love letters
scoot the north pacific gyre
clockwise,
mingle in tide charts,
kite in foam.

Double whammy fiend,
rock-a-belly earthquake
and the hard hook of wave
sluices our way.

Nehalem Bay State Park

a man in a golf cart
patrols the campground
chihuahua footprints

a black lab escapes downpour
under a metal RV
the ocean's drone

the gull watches traffic
from a light pole
mist at the boat dock

a boy scout troop bikes
the sand dune loop
slugs in ten colors

smoke from the yurt
gray lichen and yellow moss
catch the dew

rain stippled footprints
a sand trail over the dune
walk of remembrance

the old woman
hunches against wind
falling lupine seeds

Neahkahnie's mist
carded wool
in her knitter's hand

sunrise
deepens differences
in the green knitting

waves roll, churn, curve,
crest off the top
spindrift

Running the Bike Loop at Nehalem Bay State Park on a Sunday

I ate too much beach wind this week.
I choose the wooded loop under hawk swirl,
watching a weekend wind-down
of packing up pots, kites, and kids' bikes.
One left-behind firepit
smolders marshmallow smoke.

On the bike trail, huckleberries grow
cuddling up to pines.
Song sparrow melodies
dip below the ocean lullaby
to the blue lupine
and wild strawberry blooms.

Grandparents recover
on split-log benches from childcare stints.
Low tide lays bare the bayside slime flats' smell
of centuries.

On the way out, I stop at the park ranger's shack
to chew the fat about two bald eagles
circling the bay. I report the steaming ashes.

The park's flags hang limp
inside the tree buffer.

I ask why
both the U.S. and the Oregon flags
are at half-mast.

He says, "An Oregon boy died
in Afghanistan."

Heading out the only route
to a soft path through dunes,
a turn north on hard-packed beach,
a stiff wind finds my back.

Silver

A score of sanderlings scoot off,
twist as one on silver wings,
morning shine on water.
Their bellies glint
split-seconds of sunlight.

So many years I've combed
this beach. Sand slides out
under a rising ocean, bird nest and rest
places dwindle. Piper throngs
shrink. Flashing sideways like tinsel,
wondrous, but few.

Toward Neahkahnie, out of mist
as spring sun warms the sand,
a skinny man walks on mirrors,
his bald head also silver.
Sanderlings swoosh near him,
wavy reflections darting.

He comes slowly, this man of mine, reciting
the Jabberwocky from his mirrored memory.
The sanderlings flee
his bandersnatch on toothpick legs.

We stroll, a flock of two
on glass.

For Want of a Feather

That young mother grabbed a chance
to walk alone and stooped for an eagle feather
floating in a tide pool under sandstone cliffs.

She wears it back to the beach lodge –
twice the width of her head
skewering a red knot of wavy, wind-flared hair.

I almost say *you can't own that feather*,
(I wish I had found it first)
or *give it to me, I'll gift it*
to my Shoshone friend.

I am no god of feathers.
I covet it.

At dusk a lone eagle glides over
the lodge low, presenting itself to mothers
and children singing easy rounds
on the porch.

A hole gapes
in its right wing,
a window blind on a slatted whole.

The Gull

The gull lifts
 sun-warmed in noon.

You pull my hat down
over lifted eyebrows
and count on swollen fingers
birthdays, cancer-free
anniversaries, time we never believed
we had left.

South of Nehalem Bay
a black squall advances.
The gull veers off to green harbor upriver,
a white bird heading back to white boats.

If I Could Come Back

I used to imagine
coyote or crow — single-file
ants or web-weavers.

That changed in the war tide.

Now for me it's squid
   three green hearts
   long penises
   translucent ovaries
   jet-powered locomotion
   short-lived (come round again fast
   like roulette)

and ink!
   I'm out-of-here escape in ink
   no more blowhards, suicide bombers
   tyrants, bigots or pigs.

I am out of here –
   writing memoir on the sea scrolls.

Ode to the Douglas Aster in October

Change tickles my nose.
So much falls. Maple leaves.
Bluejay feathers. Promises
to rebuild the south fence
before winter.

You wild blue asters list over a bit, rain smacked.
More like a tumbled display of broken watches
than a bouquet. Blue-eyed dartboards
of weather flying on, thriving
beside a dusty gravel road.

There may be time
for a bees' last chance
to turn you into honey. Maybe.

The sun still comes in blue,
afternoon wind knows some warm.

You're a stop sign.
Drop seed for next summer,
lie down for winter.

Your lanced leaves, fringe
of bloom. You, a dropped penny
no one stoops for.

Winter

January on the Oregon coast is down time.
The beach shrinks; rain slants sideways.
Gulls hunker on roofs like yard art.
Signs on boutiques: CLOSED.
Bar business is brisk. A big-screen TV
tunes in to Blazer basketball.
Wet coats drape bar chairs. Local ales
slop on tables by a driftwood fire.
Not the time for hawking Tillamook ice cream
or begging donations for Fourth of July fireworks.

On empty beachfront houses,
shade-drawn windows are silver mirrors.
Wind surfers brave no waves today.
Joggers bundle up, lean into the south wind
and let it scoot them home north.
Dogs reluctantly keep up, both ways.

Today is a mid-January's once-in-a-while morning,
a warmer wind whispers benisons to the dune grass.
I stuff a wool hat up my sleeve. The moon is up.
So is the sun. Neither is bright over a surf mean,
glassy and green.

Come June, there'll be skeleton and bald eagle kites,
children digging moats,
dogs paddling holes,
both discovering water
as if for the first time.

Orion's Promise

He dived into that dark sea
so rare this winter
to see through to the night sky,
no undercover of fog.

This morning I opened
my eyes crusted with sleep salt
wanting to relive yesterday,
that apple-tart of February sun,
warblers reading spring's smell
in the crow's blog blast.

Overnight something rough rasped off
all leftover glint of a gold day
and cast out grunted tailings
in whiskered clouds of rain.

After all my ups and downs –
sunsets, cinched-up star belts,
mists poured by weary moon maids –
how could I believe
I could relive yesterday?

The Eye of the Tide

Is it simple aging, my lament
how the beach has drifted away?

I trace the glisten of wet past
where the tide's blue salt-eye squints,
storing up Spanish explorers' footprints,
beeswax, and that busted rainbow kite
beside the recovered return of brown pelicans
filing by.

A gull tears apart a crab's leg.
My eye out for sneaker waves.
There are no more
blue glass fishing floats.
Only syringes, fisherman's knots,
beer bottles and fireworks wrappers.

Arms Open Wide

At a rest break on this beach-front ride,
the cyclo-cross racer flings his arms
in the air as waves crash on a boulder
under his feet. Of course, he gets wet.
Of course, this photo goes on Facebook.

It's taken me years to unlock my arms
like that from tight-fisted, breast-crossed
hiding, but I've done it,
weight shifting to lean into my vortex,
hold off the rogue wave,
and flow with the one-thousand-year conveyor
that takes a single drop of water
around the globe.

I rock the cradle of stars
in my internal clock and stare below
the biker's wet spandex turned up
on bulging calves
that push so far.

What Have I To Give?

Tranquility: sea-green stone
Rootedness: dune grass in a gale
Creativity: beach combings
of sea witch hair

Seals pop up, staring in
at the dogs or us,
in a sharp wind
spending the time we took
to pleasure each other,
old ballad on a half shell.

Waves vacillate
between longing and belonging.

Can I scratch murmurs in the sand
with polished driftwood
and give you time to watch
words wash away?

How long it takes you
to see
tide's time was the treasure.

Sunset

My friend and I, hypnotized
in the last light west,
sit on the edge of Neahkahnie's cliff.

A luxury of liquid flame
melts into a skyline wave,
the night silence of gulls.

We hope for a green flash of light
crashing down, a baton
salute to choirs of ancient gods.

That photographer below stands in sand shine,
kneels, a straight line to the swallowing,
a precise last gulp of day without fire.

We creep away into a dark full
of wind-pushed trees, waved-over time,
the shore's lingering watermark.

Gravity Holds Me Hostage

Hard enough in a tai chi practice,
warrior kicks meant for chins
that go only as high as shins.

I am freighted with acquiescent nods,
stoops to the sad business of in-bound news,
pendulums in my pits, grinding ferris wheels,
my fear of heights.

On tiptoe here, I spread my crane wings white, wide, risky.
My hands fan the wind. I recall the crimson squid kite
you brought to the beach last summer, hammer head
and asking eye, undulating tentacles.

Palms to earth, I bend.

I find a way to sway, paint a rainbow green,
mimic passing cirrus clouds. My hands cup to catch
and release a drink of sunlight, bring it here,
give it away.

Hard-packed sand
pushes me up.

Ecologist on the Whale-Watching Cliff on Neahkahnie Mountain

On July 1, 2014 scientists discovered a dead female humpback
they knew near Glacier Bay in Southeastern Alaska. Named
Max, this 40-year-old whale had birthed five calves that had
three grand-calves. She died from blunt trauma to her jaws
from a collision with a ship. Scientists urge captains to slow
down in areas whales frequent.

I speak with the voice I've been given.
While crickets sing and rats gnaw,
even blindness sees the spirals of loss.
Deafness longs for songs of whales.

While crickets sing and rats gnaw,
this ache is the ache of the lone wolf who roams.
Deafness longs for the songs of whales
passing in the legions of waves.

This ache is the ache of the lone wolf who roams
wilderness named for the wildness of sly does
passing below in the legions of groves.
My palms signal the wave roll of time.

Wilderness named for the wildness of shy does.
Grace given, grace spent, for the regrowth of groves.
My palms signal the wave-roll of time
into the grunts of the law and the wind's shallow sleep.

Grace given, grace spent, for the regrowth of groves.
Even blindness sees the spirals of loss.
In the grunts of the law and the wind's shallow sleep,
I speak with the voice I've been given

to sing with whales in legions of waves.

Why I Wear Royal Purple Chicken Feathers in My Hair

Purple is the shadow of the Appaloosa mare
on the Nez Perce reservation.
Her head nods over barbed-wire, waiting
for the school bus to bring children home
to hand her ripped-up pasture grass.

Purple celebrates March's gray whale migration
high on a Neahkahnie rock wall,
binoculars to sleek backs, rolling shows.

Purple fears bloodshed, breadlines, and crime tape,
retreats into watery hymns of petition
to soften the saffron glare
when children cry with teachers from gunshots.

Purple is an underhanded wench
who hums madrigals of serpents,
sips the blue moon's spangled stars
from jelly jars, and sniffs hints
of honey, sage and lilac.

My purple is a tiny dragon, exhaling dusk,
who transforms the drool-juice of plums
into luck and forgiveness. She sneaks under my eyelids,
pinched shut against a wildfire sun over droughted plains.

Like me, she seeks home in a rock castle,
a stout fortress in blackberry brandy,
a lick of molasses, and down pillows
nestled below a stretched fall night.

July 3rd Set Up

Pick-up trucks haul in folding chairs.
Parents stretch masking tape to mark off street seats
for candy-grabbing children.

Twelve hundred chairs chain up
with orange extension cords,
caution tape twittering in the wind, and twine.

Bryar and her father pound together
a lemonade stand in the parking lot,
$1 a cup.

The biggest bunting hangs
on the mortage company porch.
The state park is a parking lot

of SUVs, mobile homes,
bikes, tents and campfires.
Teenagers eye each other.

The grocery store chalks out
a no-chairs-here warning.
The store closes during the parade

starting tomorrow at one.
On the rutted road
back up to the top of the mountain,

we bump past the four-hundred-year-old spruce
hung in worn-out moss.
The Grandmother Tree.

This, our kindred earth,
common air swept up from the beach.

The Fourth of July Parade

We swing our pick-up truck into the
library lot, settle in the truck bed,
kingpins on folding chairs.
There's a husky in a red-and-white
bandana and a bloodhound with a Statue
of Liberty crown. Sweating, paunchy
men wear goofy hats. Aging women
in sparkles guard igloo coolers.   *I want a kazoo band.*

Parades are not free-form. There are
rules. Don't throw candy at children;
it lures them into the street.   *Pony up a five-dollar*
Clean up behind horses.   *donation to enter.*

A private plane buzzes Laneda Avenue.   *It's off! Big Wigs.*
Boy Scouts wave the colors. Some   *Jabez Cleveland, my*
veterans walk. The veterans' float has   *ancestor, a fifer, died*
four empty seats. A Patriot Guardsman   *in the American*
roars his Harley. Manzanita's Citizens of   *Revolution. What did*
the Year precede the Mayor.   *Lao Tzu mean, "Rule a*
Fire & Rescue tows a trailer   *big country the way*
of jet skis and boogie boards.   *you cook a small*
  fish"?

The marching band plays
Yankee Doodle Dandy.
And riding on a pony
is the Tillamook Rodeo Queen.   *Clean up behind her*
Then Juliette, Miss Fourth of July.   *bay mare.*

A woman carries a
www.sickstarfish.com sign.   *I vote for the eight*
Grass is for Animals – the Elks drug   *maids-a-pushing book*
awareness truck. *Living Local* and the   *carts from the*

81

Tillamook County Jersey Princess.   *Tillamook Library.*

Imagine No Malaria on a lone walker.

Eight men with sunglasses and black
suits patrol beside a black convertible   *My first glance?*
carrying a man wearing an Obama mask.   *Morticians.*

Three Chinese dragons.   *The only Chinese*
A drill team twirls dragon boat oars.   *restaurant here went*
     broke years ago.

A man on a tall unicycle.   *He may be the only*
     black man in town.

A gaggle of girls carrying white   *A simple costume.*
umbrellas trailing white streamers.   *Moon jellies.*

A young girl in a motorized wheelchair   *She made my parade.*
with her panting yellow lab companion.

People who clean the street follow   *Around the all-one*
those who came before.   *earth clouds scud.*
     Here, isolated patches
     of cumulus cold-float
     over interconnected
     seas visible from the
     moon.

A free sunburn.

Letter #33 to Manzanita City Council

This is my last water bill payment — I'm selling my house on Beeswax. Thank you again for asking for citizen comment.

The City did a fine job coordinating the Fourth of July parade today. Thousands of people contributed to the local economy and enjoyed the heat.

May I ask the City to require next year that the vintage cars in the parade display signs identifying the make of the car and date of manufacture? Many viewers were left guessing.

Ask drivers to include exhaust emission numbers and the average mileage per gallon on highway and in-town driving. While I admire the shine and retro-style of antique cars, including this information would educate our children and grandchildren. They will deal with the consequences of greenhouse gas emissions for the rest of their lives. They should know.

You request that equestrians shovel up after their horses. Insist drivers own up to what autos leave in the ocean air.

Thank you.

The Ring of Fire from Fire Mountain

Evening of July Fourth

From the top of Neahkahnie at nine o'clock
sixty-five bonfires are visible on the beach.

Impatience launches fire crackers,
fountains, mortars, and spinners,
as far down the beach as we can see –
past Manzanita, Brighton, Rockaway,
maybe as far as Garibaldi.
Screamer rockets back up the scorched
red and gold chrysanthemums.
Blasts reverberate up the rock.

A one-thousand-foot radius circle in the sand
is cordoned off for contracted fireworks
starting at ten. Exactly then.

Thirty-eight minutes of rockets.
Up, up. Out over the ocean. Motley gold flames
birth from the drizzled glitter of each last sizzle.

Sky-flowers bloom and boom above the whale road.
Smoke bunches into a black cloud
at the base of the mountain.
The winds blow it east to the forest.

I know the nightfall-fate
of those living fireworks,
plover, gull and cormorant.

The Shattered Visage of the Wilderness Act

After Percy Bysshe Shelley

The shattered visage of the Wilderness Act
lies buried ear-up in rippled tide-sands
listening for fractures. A sparkler wire pierces
its eyeball socket black with burn.

The holiday star-works of a bombing nation
burst open a war zone. This is hangover.

A row of cottage windows on the beach berm
mirror the fading sun. Dune grass buffers
the way to the beach. Then sand.
Hear water folding, sand accepting,
tides daring and undoing.

Here no goal posts, putting greens,
restrooms, sites for campers, trees planted
for posterity, a rocky trail to a ferny waterfall,
no landmarks to passages of tribes.

This is the shape-shifting of solitude.
I hug the man next to me but in this wind
never feel his breath.
Footprints and tire tracks dissolve.

The gulls, pelicans, cormorants,
pigeon guillemots, murres, terns, and shearwaters
turn from rest, from nests. The whales hear,
seals puzzle over hoots at melting sky-flowers.

Blasts of mortars and screamers do not honor
birds who own this sky,
the fish outside the dead-zones.
Inalienable rights are not indelible.

Can the west wind blow back awe?
Will slumbering crust insist
on up-thrust, side-slip, deluge?

How long until the storm crushes
that colossal wreck of a conqueror's sneer
where the sands stretch far away?

No Smoking Gun

Those are the fire chief's words,
July 8, 2014 at 6 p.m.

Wind from the south fanned up ten-foot flames
from smoldering driftwood on boulders
at the base of Neahkahnie.

A bonfire incompletely doused,
maybe seething for days,
until gusts brought it to life again.

Forty-five firefighters pulled out hoses.
Neighbors with buckets and shovels
threw sand on flames

which leaped up the steep hillside,
grabbed stunted trees and gold grasses
and singed four vacant
bleach-shingled ocean-front second homes,
each with a full horizon view of ocean.

At ten p.m., responders went home.
For the time being

there is a ban on open burning,
a change in the rules
when money burns.

No smoking gun,

this bonfire in silver driftwood
where wind lifts fire higher
than the tide.

The Wind Sees Us and the Sea

You are the landlocked
who stand on the shore
in sieved rains. I breathe
at you.

Your bodies and boats are eggshells
that pile up like driftwood on the jetty.
Sea-smoothed sticks fit human palms
like guns. My firepower naps
in the sea's tides until I rouse.

The ocean's nursery cradle-rocks
this salty edge. You beings crawl
late to the crèche, having forgotten
caution first,
slithering second.

This water is a graveyard
under green-glass waves
that buries the silts, the sea-witched,
and the sweepings you jettison
to lighten listing, dangerous loads.

My storm gales roil up mountains
in the surf. You run east,
slogging through soft sand
for high ground

as if your dust,
paper, scissors, stones,
and ancient mud are fortresses
safe from the claws
I glad-hand to the sea.

On the Cliff with Your Ashes

Mom – I'm here, on a damp fir log on the basalt cliff
over Devil's Cauldron, behind three slanted pines
that fence off the verge, enough timber
to keep my head from swimming.

Why so long to come back to this rim?
Why so long to fight the fish net
you cast, the one I hacked out of with steel
scissors, cold in my hand like sliver shivs?

Have pelted rains and ocean waves
rinsed your ashes off this rock?
If I tossed a pebble, would it ricochet
off atoms of your skull and shoulder blades?

You hangered in re-enforced rib bone.
The Depression gave you a typewriter.
I had universities and my own black car.
We seldom talked our way inside rough edges.

We learned there's good enough, maybe
never enough, and the whole works for less.
You told my father – either a job or another baby.
He said another baby. Me.

You were eight when women voted. You stood up
to the DAR to give that award to the Cherokee girl.
When your belly bloated, you called it an abdominal tumor.
We rolled you to the polling booth in a wheel chair to vote
for death with dignity. Your death certificate – ovarian cancer,
ovary not a word you spoke.

Your ashes on this scarp.
This fog smells of fir needles

and wild mushrooms.
I miss your Chanel.
How long it took me to get back here.

Longer yet to the breakers below.
When there's even fewer fish to catch,
my ash will join yours.
Here. Where eagles grab hold
to face a subducted, precarious west.

My Memory Is a Minus Tide

It seeps out
to where fishing boats teeter
on slimy rocks.

The sun yellows its slow caution
and wave caps drag down
the names I've forgotten for common

flaxseed and fuchsias,
the woman's nickname I stood beside
waving on the library corner

when the Dalai Lama's limo
slow-motioned down 10th to another sea.
Or those dolls we made from columns

of some floozied flower
flaunting pink petal skirts.
What I called my black Volkswagen.

These float in treasure trunks
of swaying sea weeds
a long haul from my dune.

Sand will know when the tide turns
to give me back another minute,
a high tide secret

with all its consequences.

My Windowpane

I washed this picture window the first time
to wipe away the nose smears
of the dog no longer alive.

The second time I rubbed off
lines of sun-dazzled rainbows
on almost-clean panes.

The third time I listened for the squeak
of clarity, rag on glass,
and saw through the pane
my peace rose in perfect bloom.

The Dead Warbler on My Welcome Mat

Birds can't all be trapped in angles of sun by a picture
window, open gawk of ailing, bent. Nor smudging the beach
where gulls rip shorebirds into sand-dredged shreds.

Or some dead ones that news people exploit
to hype West Nile. Crows do not pile up
like ashes in the fireplace, mourned once
under a hovering circle of black concern,
then abandoned. Some cat-prides,
woe-be-gotten, dropped on a feather
comforter or buried under lilacs.

We don't smell bird death in the scent of spring lofted
in feathers, tenderness of twigs and beetles unfolding.
Cold bird eyes have seen wood smoke flee
chimneys, mirages of heat on highway.

There must be a place where small bird song
welcomes dimming dusk and simple sadness,
last lamented landings blanketed in jaded moss.
Flight is not the immortality that angels wrestle,
winds beyond the reach of wrens.
I know there is an end.

Where they go to die
must be somewhere
I'd like to go.

My Cottage Garden after the For-Sale Sign Goes Up

I know the close hold
of a sprawl of false
lilies of the valley, a pink rose
weaving in a listing cedar fence
between me and the neighbors
whose names I never knew.

Oh, this boudoir of lace-cap hydrangea,
frilly pink and cream rhodies,
up for grabs after decades
of my picking pebbles to line the garden path,
sipping martinis teetered on the warped picnic table.
How many meals did I eat here?

A sun-bleached green-wing macaw,
rescue bird of balsa wood, is screwed
onto the strawberry tree above a bird bath
rank with rotting leaves.
How often have we yackety-yacked,
that bird and I?

My dog's paw print carved in spring mud,
everywhere my fingerprints.

Apologies to the Former Owners of My Beach House

For the odor, first I blamed the husband
who died in the house, a heart attack
volunteer fire fighters could not arrest.
The smell hung in the living room
like an invisible sack of dead fish
in the only spot with an ocean view.

Next I charged his widow. I'd met her
when my mother and I came to measure the rooms.
When my mother told her she lived in a high-rise
for seniors, the widow arched her back,
said she would never live in an old people's home
and felt sorry for my mother.

My mother smoothed the pleat of a window blind.
She loved bridge games, ladies' lunches, knitting group.
I wrote the old lady off as mean, a rotten crab.

For months I assaulted that odor.
I sniffed carpeting on my hands and knees.
Sprayed aerosol scents of white cotton laundry and fresh oranges.
Burned sage. Brewed pots of stand-up coffee. Mumbled
incantations of trance and chant, homemade exorcism.

Then I smelled wet ash, green pennies, and spent star-gazer lilies.
I spoke aloud of naming the house Ocean Pines, how we love
this home as the widow had. The wee garden.
I begged that smell to be well and to leave.
Demand, compassion, and supplication. Three scripts.
Soon it did. We claimed the sweet salt of ocean ozone.

Sand-scoured decades later, I offer the house for sale.
I can still point to where she hung, watched waves
as a dead fish tumbles in the turbulence.
The new owners shall find a spray
of yellow roses without thorns in a clear glass bowl.
I get it. Here and hereafter.

From Blue to Gray

A couple in Saudi Arabia made an offer
on Ocean Pines. Realtors brought the papers.
A house with history, some lead paint,
an uncertain woodstove, probably some rot.

I know where the emergency candles wait,
the whine of the kitchen exhaust fan,
the rumbled letting-down of ice cubes,
which friend of my mother's
sold me that glass lamp.

Generations of children
have built dams in the outflow creek
at the foot of Beeswax Lane.
I cleaned St. Helens' ash from the gutters.

Watched life-flight helicopters on rescue missions
and military planes scope the coast.
Paid twice as much for flood insurance
as annual property taxes.
Three of the dogs I brought here
are dead. Mother's ashes on Neahkahnie.

Here I learned the blues,
greens, grays, blacks,
phosphorescent silvers, golds,
tans, and whites of the Pacific Ocean.

A pressure ridge forms on my index finger
as I initial every page of the sales binder
in jet black ink.

Man Cleaning Closet

He languishes
lacking order and interest.
Lackadaisical

like an archaeologist
on vacation from university
digging clams and broken sea glass.

He avoids halting remainders
of worn shoe soles, bits of flint and frass,
sand dumped from cuffs.

He tries to secure a village of remnants
in a cardboard box between jousts with dust bunnies,
acknowledging his compulsions about space.

He found the wedding ring
from my first marriage
just in time, he says, for lunch.

Wiping Up for Moving Out

I wipe cabinet shelves with a damp rag, mop up bits of faded rosemary and dry parsley. Hand you the scallop shell nightlight. Find a forgotten Swiss Army knife with a corkscrew in a mildewed leather holster — that would be his, the man before you. A flat refrigerator magnet says Wisconsin, a tenant's. Stuff the West Coast bird books into a cardboard stereo box. Sniff the olive oil, how old is gone? Save the rusted pruning shears. Wonder if the new owners will regulate the pink climbing rose or let its thorns grab their sweaters. I hope they like blue. The robin-egg blue garage, new Yale blue carpeting. A rivulet of groundwater from the sump pump flows down the gutter toward the corner of Carmel and Beeswax.

In bubble wrap you cushion the print of the mother whale lifting up her baby. In a towel, I swaddle that Japanese woodblock of a tsunami wave curling under a peach sunset. We toss the surge protector into a Hood River apple box beside the stack of plastic blue and white Chinese restaurant plates and bowls my daughter wants. Pack the car. Separate out five keys for the realtors. Call our dog.

I think the tide is ebbing. My back is to the window; I do not turn to check. We're heading up, around the mountain.

> the monarch kite
> dips in sultry winds
> reeling in

Like So Many

Rain raps on the flashing,
Kona coffee brews.
A squall passes through.
My last days here are like so many.

My run on the beach
under the invocation of hail
to move faster, call the dog closer,
ends on an empty beach.
Five round crabbing floats stranded
at the high water mark of last night's storm.
April is bowling strikes
at my wind-watered eyes.

The very last day is unlike any other.
Keys to small cabinets handed over,
shelves emptied of the leashes of dead dogs,
my binoculars and a tidetable
from 2006, the three-tiered rainbow kite
that crashes headfirst after a one-minute sail
tucked into the trunk of the car.

Next days like no others.
Acid water. Dead zones.
Changed winds. High waters.
Fickle currents.
Tsunami. Who knows
how the earth shifts
its wounds?

I'm not off to something more,
maybe something less. Close my eyes

to the mountain in mist.
The smell of a well-loved house
on a salt-rimed sea
I take with me.

There Will Be Wave Walkers

Sea-caress sounds draw us
to the rushing in place, the balance
of menace in reigning winds,
the susurrus of solitude.

After my old house
is washed out to sea, rattled to timbers,
and the shore finds its next shape,
there will be walkers, wave watchers.

Notes

Mise en Scène. Sources for this prose poem include NOAA, population studies, voting records and tourist information websites. The map is courtesy of Elk Ridge Publishing, Manzanita, Oregon.

"Dead zones" off the Oregon coast are no secret. Scientists have identified then since 2002. Find information in "Hypoxia: How Is It Affecting Ocean Life, and Why?" by Nathan Gilles, Oregon Sea Grant, 2012, Oregon State University.

"Geoarchaeology of the Nehalem Spit: Redistribution of Beeswax Galleon Wreck Debris by Cascadia Earthquake and Tsunami (1700 A.D)", by Curt D. Peterson, Scott S. Williams, Kenneth M. Cruikshank,and John R. Dubè appeared in *Geoarchaeology: An International Journal*, Vol. GEO. 26, No. 2. The article describes the impact of the 1700 A. D. tsunami on shipwreck debris deposited on Manzanita's beaches before the tsunami. The Pacific Northwest Seismic Network's (PNSN) website uses the phrase "locked and loaded" to refer to the Cascadia subduction zone — as do dozens of other scientific, policy and media websites. *The Next Tsunami – Living on a Restless Coast* (Bonnie Henderson, Oregon State University Press, 2014) shares scientific acknowledgement of the impact of the 1700 A.D. earthquake and the threat of the Cascadia Subduction Zone to produce another 9-plus scale earthquake.

A rich source for first-people stories about the area surrounding Nehalem Bay and Neahkahnie Mountain is *Nehalem Tillamook Tales*, recorded by Elizabeth Derr Jacobs and edited by Melville Jacobs, University of Oregon Books, Eugene, Oregon, 1959.

Lines from Kahlil Gibran's poetry are from *Sand and Foam*, Alfred A. Knopf, New York, 1969, p. 1.

The Way the Wind Blows. D. W. Johnson's essay "Shore Processes" and "Shoreline Development" is in *The Book of the Sea,* Appleton-Century-Crofts, Inc. New York, 1954, p. 281.

Klaska **– The Lost Clatsop Word for** *They.* Information concerning the languages and legends of the Clatsop and Nehalem Bay tribes came from *Ten Years in Oregon*, by D. Lee and J. H. Frost, first published in 1844 by J. Collord Printer. The Commission on Archives and History Oregon-Idaho Conference, United Methodist Church copied the report in 1994.

The Wreck of the Santo Cristo De Burgos on Manzanita Beach

(1693). Information about efforts to locate the wreck of the Santo Cristo De Burgos is on the website of The Beeswax Wreck Project. The site details how beeswax from the galleon washed up over many decades onto Manzanita's shores. It was this beeswax that the poet's street, Beeswax Lane, was named for. The poet is grateful to Scott Williams, the Principal Investigator of the Beeswax Wreck Project and an archaeologist with the Washington State Department of Transportation, for his help.

Tales of the Neahkahnie Treasure contains photos of beeswax found at Manzanita and of rock carvings on Neahkahnie that treasure seekers hope point to buried gold from Spanish galleons. The Nehalem Valley Historical Society Treasure Committee prepared the pamphlet in 1991.

Driftwood. Current research documents how accumulations of driftwood benefit beach ecology. Driftwood traps sand on beaches, stabilizes coastal dunes, and protects cliffs from erosion. Floating or sunken driftwood provides habitat and food in the deep-sea. *From the Forest to the Sea — the Ecology of Wood in Streams, Rivers, Estuaries and Oceans* by Chris Maser and James R. Sedell (St. Lucie Press, 1994) focuses on the importance of driftwood accumulations on the shores of the Pacific Northwest.

As for Shopping. Thank you, Kathleen Ryan and Mark Beach, for good humored help preparing this list of what's available in Manzanita and what is not. Ryan and Beach are long-time residents of Manzanita.

The Refindery. Lines from Lewis Carroll's *Through the Looking Glass* are requoted from *The Book of Fabulous Beasts*, by Joseph Nigg, 1999, Oxford University Press, p. 326.

Mid-Week Mid-Morning May. The last line of this poem is from Pablo Neruda's *The Book of Questions*, Copper Canyon Press, 1974, translated by William O'Daly, p. 39.

Blessing the Fleet. Since 1981, around Memorial Day, the community of Garibaldi, Oregon (seventeen miles south of Manzanita) holds a Blessing of the Fleet. The ceremony begins at the Coast Guard Memorial near the U. S. Coast Guard Rescue Station. After acknowledging those who have lost their lives at sea and saying prayers for the safety of those going to sea in the coming season, community members are invited onto fishing boats. The boats follow a Coast Guard vessel into Tillamook Bay to cast flowers on the waters.

Sand Script. A line from Rachel Carson's *Under the Sea-Wind* inspired *Sand Script:* "In the hollows of the dunes the beach grasses lean in the wind and with their pointed tips write endless circles in the sand." From *The Book of the Sea*, edited by A. C. Spectorsky, Appleton-Century-Crofts, Inc., New York, 1954, p. 292.

Vellella vellella. Sometimes tens of thousands of these tiny hydroid polyps commonly known as "by-the-wind sailors" strand on shores from British Columbia to California. They are the size of the bottom of a jelly jar and look like blue translucent, fragile paper. Individuals come in two forms. Think "lefties" and "righties" — some with sails (clear standing-up parts) that slant from left to right and others with sails from right to left. The sails stay 45 degrees to the wind. The direction of the sail determines where the wind takes them – either Japan or the West Coast. They float on the surface until the tide casts them up on beaches to die.

Sea Stars. Scientists know "star-wasting disease" is happening up and down the Pacific Coast in larger geographic areas than ever before and in greater numbers, but not exactly why. See information on star wasting disease added to the webpages of the *Pacific Rocky Intertidal Monitoring: Trends and Synthesis* of the University of California Santa Cruz website in September 2013.

The Gray Whale. Gray whales continue to die or suffer from consuming ocean trash. Joy Primrose, the Oregon representative of the American Cetacean Society, said in a note to the poet, "Gray Whales migrate to the breeding and calving lagoons in Baja California, Mexico. The majority of the whales migrate to arctic feeding grounds. However, the Pacific Coast Feeding Group are about 200 Gray Whales that spend the summer and fall feeding from Northern California to British Columbia. These are the whales we see off Oregon in summer and fall. Winter migration along the Oregon Coast usually runs mid-December to mid-January with the northbound migration along Oregon usually mid-March through May."

The Big If on Nehalem Bay Spit. Western Snowy Plovers are about the size of a sparrow. Their habitat is on sandy areas above high tide with limited vegetation. They are nearly the color of sand. In 1993 the U. S. Fish & Wildlife Service listed the population as threatened. Years ago they nested in twenty-nine locations along Oregon's shores. Now eight locations support nesting populations. The snowy plover nesting season runs from March through September — prime time for tourist activity on Oregon beaches. On April 3, 2015, a wildlife biologist spotted one pair nesting at Nehalem Bay State Park.

After the Storm That Took the Power Out. Oregon's Administrative Rules (OAR) determine when and where people may harvest beach logs. The restrictions tend to be narrow rather than "free for all." At non-state park beaches, driftwood removal is to be hand lifted rather than loaded with a machine. A person may be permitted to take up to three cords of wood per calendar year and may use chainsaws. The OAR states, "A person may not disturb, cut, mutilate or remove ancient tree stumps, including but not limited to those found on the ocean shore state recreation area at the Neskowin ghost forest." Wood embedded in sand cannot be removed. At State Parks, visitors may take souvenirs or gifts. The State may issue permits for wood gathering. Only a handful of rangers patrol the Oregon coast. Jurisdictions such as the City of Manzanita may help with the support of law enforcement officers to oversee driftwood harvesting.

Letter #32 to City Council. During World War II all bonfires were prohibited on Oregon's beaches following the Western Defense Command's 1942 Public Proclamation to provide "dim out" security. Oregon Parks and Recreation now manages regulations related to campfires on Oregon beaches. They are to be in open, dry sand away from dune grass, vegetation and beach log and driftwood accumulations. They may not be larger than three feet by three feet without a special permit. There is little enforcement of these regulations.

Tsunami Sea Glass. As of 2014, most of the debris from the 2011 Japanese earthquake and tsunami has sunk — or is spread out over an ocean area several times the size of the United States. Much of it did come ashore on the west coast, however, including Manzanita.

Running the Bike Loop at Nehalem Bay State Park on a **Sunday.** Spc. Brandon J. Prescott, age 24, of Bend, Oregon died on May 4, 2013 in the Maiwand District of Kandahar Province in Afghanistan, a victim of an improvised roadside bomb. This poem was written on May 5, 2013.

Silver. Oregon State University (OSU) has released information about increasing wave height in the Pacific Ocean. OSU scientists are modeling how intensifying El Nino events and wave heights, along with higher sea levels, may impact lowland flooding and beach erosion. Brian Fagan's *The Attacking Ocean — The Past, Present and Future of Rising Sea Levels* (Bloomsbury Press, 2013) details the global impacts of rising sea levels, storm-caused sea surges, earthquakes and tsunamis.

The Sanderling is on the American Bird Conservancy U. S. 2007 Watchlist of Concern.

The Douglas Aster in October. The ubiquitous purple-blue wild aster is in full glory at the Oregon coast in October. Like the Douglas fir, it is named for the eighteenth-century naturalist from Scotland, David Douglas, who traveled the Pacific Northwest keeping a journal from 1823 to 1827.

The Fourth of July Parade. The quotation from Lao Tzu is from Ursula Leguin's translation of the *Tao Te Ching: A Book About the Way and the Power of the Way*, Lao Tzu, Shambala, 1997.

The Ring of Fire from Fire Mountain. The Fireworks policy of the Oregon Department of Parks and Recreations is crystal clear: "Personal use of fireworks in the parks and on the beaches is prohibited. Explosives, fireworks or other substances that could cause harm are not allowed. Fireworks are prohibited in Oregon State Parks and Ocean Shores, including sparklers."

Other ocean-front locales — San Diego and Monterey Bay as examples — study how fireworks affect marine mammals and shorebirds and regulating firework blasts. U.S. Fish & Wildlife issued a report that Oregon shorebirds in an area south of Manzanita leave nesting areas within minutes of detonations. And possibly abandon their nests.

The Shattered Visage of the Wilderness Act. The Wilderness Act of 1964 set criteria for determining what comprises wilderness on tracts of federal land. In *Orion Magazine*'s September/October 2014 issue, Terry Tempest William's essay "The Glorious Indifference of Wilderness" said, "This is wilderness, to walk in silence. This is wilderness, to calm the mind. This is wilderness, my return to composure." This poet believes coastal lands meet criteria established for other kinds of wilderness. They are roadless. Untrammeled. Provide solitude. They are landscapes we cannot dominate but that we can harm. Here wind, storms and tides hold the upper hand.

No Smoking Gun. Details about this fire came from *The North Coast Citizen*, July 24, 2014, reports from people in Manzanita, and *The Daily Astorian*'s article, "Beach Grass and Driftwood Blazes Can Spread Fast," posted online on July 22, 2014.

About the Author

Tricia Knoll is an Oregon poet. For twenty-five years she owned a vacation rental in Manzanita, Oregon. *Ocean's Laughter* records years of witness to environmental change on the coast and her love of this small town with a wide outlook on the Pacific Ocean.

She moved to the West Coast in 1972. For eight years she taught high school English in Portland. Then she served as the Public Relations Director of the Portland Children's Museum. In 2007 she retired as the Public Information Director of the Portland Water Bureau. For the month of October 2005, she lived in New Orleans as part of a Portland Water Bureau response to help restore water service following Hurricane Katrina. The Portland crews lived in tents on a New Orleans Water and Sewer Board water tank site that had not flooded. She is FEMA-trained in emergency response communications. She picked up debris in Manzanita that floated onto the shore from the tsunami following the Fukishima earthquake in 2011.

Knoll's poetry has appeared in numerous journals and anthologies. Her chapbook *Urban Wild* (Finishing Line Press, 2014) focuses on the interactions of humans and wildlife in urban habitat.

She is an avid gardener of vegetables, roses and plants native to the Pacific Northwest. Knoll writes haiku, dances, runs and hula hoops as daily practices. She has run hundreds of miles on Manzanita's beach.

Knoll has degrees in literature from Stanford University (B.A.) and Yale University (M.A.T.) She is grateful to the many poets with whom she has studied and from whom she received encouragement.

Website: triciaknoll.com